W9-BHF-073

ROBOT MATH

GAMES, ACTIVITIES, AND WORKSHEETS FOR EARLY LEARNERS

Written and Illustrated by Patricia Rex

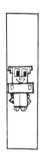 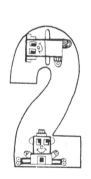 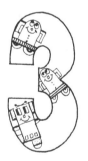 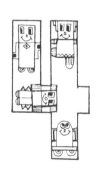 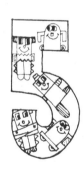

Fearon Teacher Aids
a division of
David S. Lake Publishers
Belmont, California

Designer: Susan Pinkerton

Entire contents copyright © 1989 by David S. Lake
Publishers, 500 Harbor Boulevard, Belmont, California
94002. However, the individual purchaser may reproduce
designated materials in this book for classroom and
individual use, but the purchase of this book does not entitle
reproduction of any part for an entire school, district, or
system. Such use is strictly prohibited.

ISBN 0-8224-5841-1

Printed in the United States of America

1. 9 8 7 6 5 4 3 2 1

Contents

Introduction

My robot books began as supplemental activities that I developed for my kindergarten classes. Many children in my classes needed additional activities using shapes, and I began to create activities to fill that need. The children enjoyed these robot-theme activities so much that I expanded the theme into other areas of the curriculum.

Robot Math offers worksheets, games, and activities that help children learn basic math skills: number recognition, number values, number sequence, and simple addition. The math games and activities give children hands-on experience in counting, adding, and expressing number values. Detailed instructions and patterns are provided for the games.

The forty-two reproducible math worksheets include cut-and-paste, color-by-number, dot-to-dot, and other popular formats. These worksheets develop skills in recognizing numbers, number values, and number sequence.

A special Marshmallow Robots section provides instructions on how to help students create robots out of large and small marshmallows. These robots are useful for practice in counting, adding, and other activities. The Marshmallow Robot Design Cards and Adding Cards give students additional practice in math skills.

You may want to display the robots your students create, along with colorful robot room decorations. I have found that using a robot theme in my classroom is a fun and rewarding experience for both my students and myself. I hope you will enjoy using this theme in your own classroom.

Robot Games

The following robot games provide practice in number values and counting. They are simple to make, fun to play, and easy to learn.

Stack Robots

Materials
Colored construction paper
Scissors
Markers
Stack Robot patterns (page 8)
Storage container such as a file folder

Procedure
Determine which numerals you wish to include in the game. For each numeral, you will need one Robot Head and one Robot Wheels pattern. Duplicate the patterns on colored construction paper and cut them out.

If you are studying numbers 1 to 5, cut out fifteen $1\frac{1}{2}'' \times 1\frac{1}{2}''$ squares of colored construction paper. If you are studying numbers 6 to 10, cut out forty $1\frac{1}{2}'' \times 1\frac{1}{2}''$ squares. If you are studying numbers 1 to 10, cut out fifty-five $1\frac{1}{2}'' \times 1\frac{1}{2}''$ squares.

On each Robot Wheels pattern, write a number. Laminate the Robot Wheels, Robot Heads, and squares for durability. The pieces may be stored in a file folder that has been taped on two sides to form a pocket. Label the file folder with the name of the game.

Directions to the Child

"These are parts for the stack robots. Make the robots by naming the numeral on the bottom part and stacking that many squares above the number. Add a head on top." You may want to add, "Then put the stack robots in order."

Robot Knobs

Materials

Construction paper or tagboard
Markers
Robot patterns (page 9)
Counters (buttons, old knobs, milk jug lids, or anything durable, safe, and round)
Storage box (plastic shoe box or cigar box)

Procedure

Duplicate the robot patterns on construction paper or tagboard. You will need one robot pattern for each number you wish to include. Decorate and outline the robots with markers. Print one numeral on each robot. Laminate the robots for durability.

Label the storage box. Fill it with the appropriate number of counters.

robots numbered 1 to 5—15 counters needed
robots numbered 6 to 10—40 counters needed
robots numbered 1 to 10—55 counters needed

Directions to the Child

"The robots have lost their knobs. Help each robot find the correct number of knobs by naming its numeral and counting that many knobs. Put the correct number of knobs on each robot."

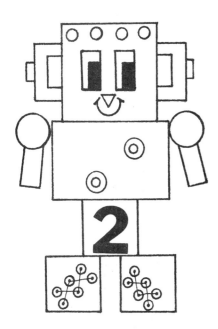
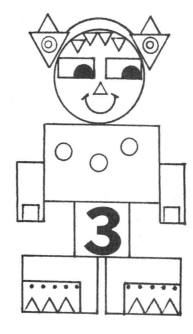

Counting Robots

Materials
A favorite number pattern (1 to 10) to be enlarged
Colored construction paper
Robot patterns (page 10)
Scissors
Markers
Storage box such as a shoe box

Procedure
Enlarge the numerals in your favorite number pattern to the desired size (to fit in the storage box). Laminate and cut out the numerals.

Duplicate the robot patterns on construction paper to make counters. Decorate them with markers, laminate them, and cut them out.

Directions to the Child
"See how many robots each number will hold. Put one robot on the numeral one. Put two robots on the numeral two. Continue until all the numerals have the correct number of robots. Which numeral holds the most robots? Which one is most crowded?"

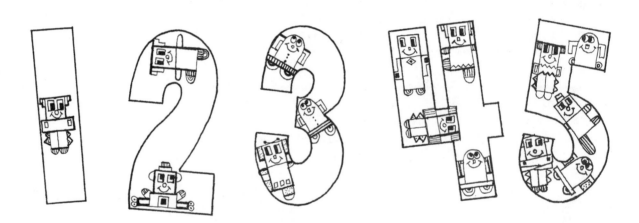

Robot Room Decorations

For a fun room decoration that illustrates number values, enlarge your favorite number pattern to 12 inches or more. Duplicate the numerals on colored construction paper and cut them out. Make the robot counters according to the instructions in "Counting Robots." Glue the robot counters to the numerals. Laminate the numerals. Pin the decorations to a wall.

The children will be able to tell at a glance the number of items that each numeral "holds." Larger numerals will be crowded with robots, and smaller numerals will be less crowded.

You may also use the patterns on pages 8–10 to create your own bulletin boards and robot math posters.

Marshmallow Robot Activities

Marshmallow Robots offer a whimsical, fun approach to counting, adding, and constructing. Students begin with a memorable counting activity—making a simple marshmallow robot—and then progress to more complex jobs.

Introductory Activity

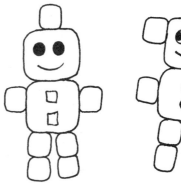

Materials
Large and small marshmallows
Toothpicks
Decorations (small buttons, brads, etc.)
Colored construction paper
Hole punch
Glue
Wiggly eyes (optional)

Procedure
Provide each student with two large marshmallows and two small marshmallows, toothpicks, decorations, and construction paper. Remind students not to eat the marshmallows, and set guidelines for using the toothpicks safely.

Tell the students, "Today we will make robots out of marshmallows. Because we will be gluing eyes and buttons on these marshmallows, we cannot eat them. On another day, we may make special robots to decorate and eat."

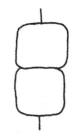

Demonstrate how to make a simple marshmallow robot. Say, "Stick a toothpick through the big marshmallows. This is the body of the robot. How many big marshmallows are there? (*Two.*)"

"Next, find the small marshmallows. Push a toothpick through the large marshmallow on the bottom. Put a small marshmallow on each end of the toothpick. These are the robot's arms. How many small marshmallows are there? (*Two.*) How many marshmallows altogether? (*Four.*)"

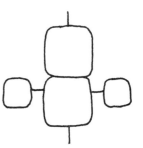

Let the children use construction paper, buttons, and so on, to decorate their robots. Use a hole punch on colored construction paper to make dots for the robots' eyes. (Wiggly eyes may also be used.)

When the robots are complete, review how they are made. Give each child a piece of paper. Say, "Count how many big marshmallows we used in the robot. There is a number you can write to tell how many there are. Write how many big marshmallows there are. (2) Now, write how many small marshmallows there are. (2) Now, write how many marshmallows there are altogether. (4)"

When the children are familiar with this concept, you may introduce the Marshmallow Robot Design Cards and Adding Cards. Robot marshmallow activities may be used throughout the year as learning center games or as teacher-directed counting jobs.

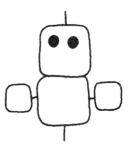

Tips
- Ask parents to send marshmallows from time to time.
- Use colored marshmallows for variety.
- For an open house activity, display student work. Exhibit the marshmallow robots.
- For edible robots, add chocolate chips, candy sprinkles, cake decorations, whipped cream, etc.
- Reuse marshmallows as counters. The marshmallows harden, but they don't mold. When they look undesirable, replace them.

Marshmallow Robot Design Cards

The Marshmallow Robot Design Cards (pages 53–55) may be used in several different ways. Duplicate the cards on white contruction paper, laminate them, and cut them apart.

Uses

- Give each child a Robot Design Card. Provide marshmallows, toothpicks, large wiggly eyes, and glue. Have the children look at their cards and construct robots that match the cards. Show children who have difficulty constructing the robots how to put marshmallows on top of the card before assembling the robots. Help each student draw a mouth on the robot with a felt-tipped pen.

- Laminate the cards twice to make wipe-off cards. Have the students count the marshmallows (large and small) needed to make each robot and write the numbers on the card. Store the cards in a labeled plastic bag or file folder, along with wipe-off crayons or grease pencils and rags.

- For a small group activity, give each child one or more cards along with a blank piece of paper. Have the children count the number of marshmallows (large and small) needed to make the robot and write the numbers on the piece of paper. Students can then exchange cards and repeat the activity. Go over the correct answers with the children or let them check each other's answers.

- Cut white felt pieces into marshmallow shapes. Have the children arrange the shapes on a flannel board to copy the robots on the cards. Or, glue a magnet or a magnetic strip on the felt shapes and let the children create the robots on a metal filing cabinet or other metal surface.

Marshmallow Robot Adding Cards

The Marshmallow Robot Adding Cards (pages 56–60) may be used for different purposes.

Uses:
- Duplicate the Adding Cards and use them as color-and-count worksheets. Students can count the number of large and small marshmallows and write the numbers below to complete the equation.

- Laminate the Adding Cards twice to make a learning center wipe-off game. Store the cards in a box with wipe-off crayons or grease pencils, and rags or old socks. Label the box and write simple instructions on it for the children.

- Provide marshmallows for the children and let them stack marshmallows on the Adding Card equation to find the sum.

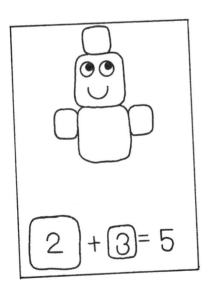 

Robot Heads

Robot Wheels

Stack Robots

Robot Math © 1989 David S. Lake Publishers

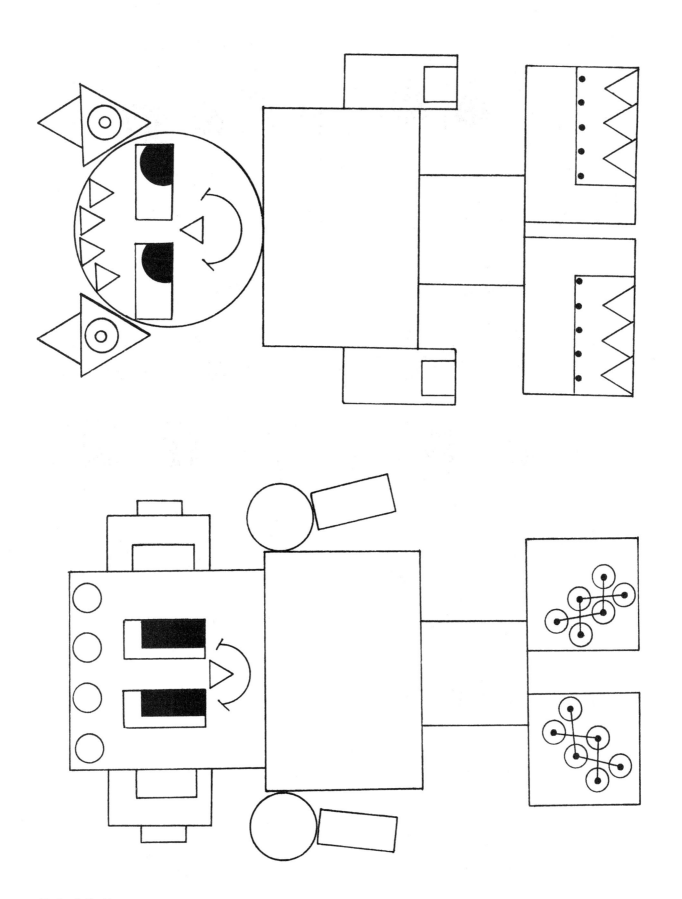

Robot Patterns

Robot Math © 1989 David S. Lake Publishers

Name _____

Count the dots on each robot. Cut out the pieces below.
Match and paste them to the robots.

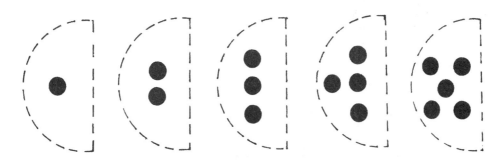

Robot Math © 1989 David S. Lake Publishers   Identifying Same-Number Sets **11**

Count the triangles on each robot. Cut out the circles.
Match and paste them to the robots.

Robot Math © 1989 David S. Lake Publishers

Count the dots on each robot's head. Cut out the rectangles. Match and paste them to the robots.

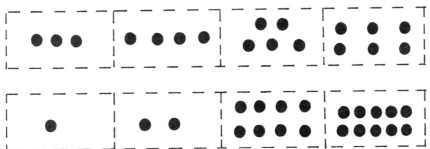

Count the robots in each set. Circle the number that tells how many there are.

Robot Math © 1989 David S. Lake Publishers

Name _____

Count the robots in each set. Cut out and then paste the number that tells how many there are.

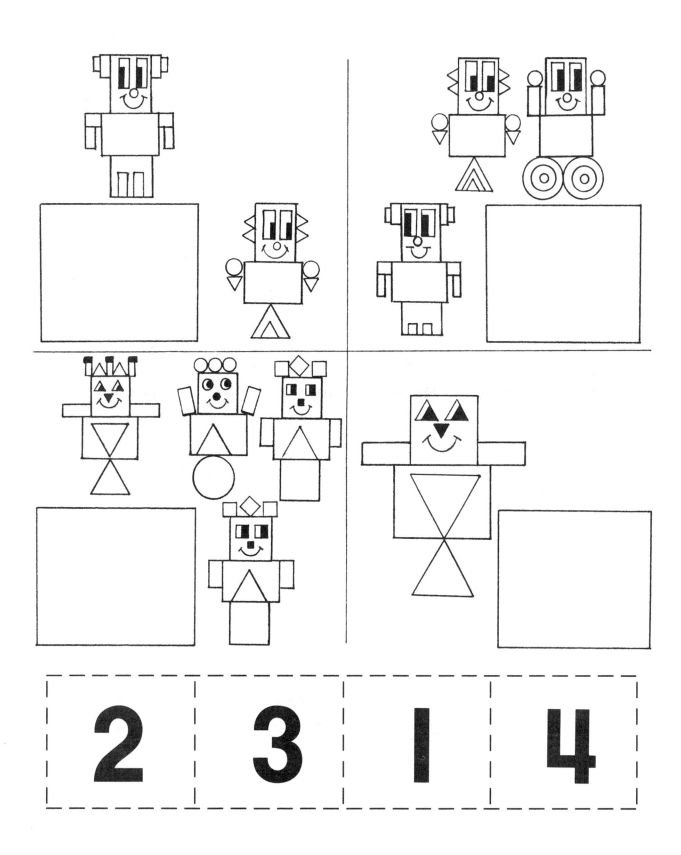

Name _____

Look at the number on each robot. Color the correct number of squares.

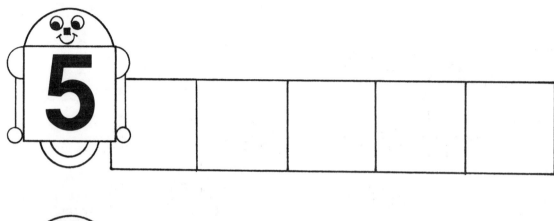

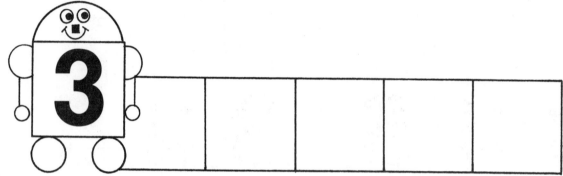

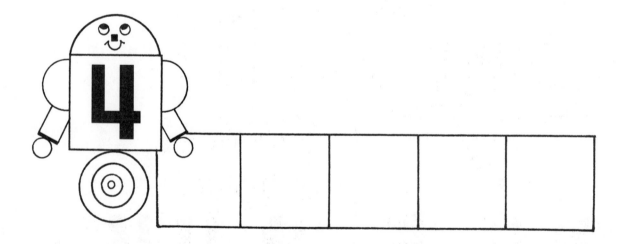

Robot Math © 1989 David S. Lake Publishers

Name _____

Count the robots in each set. Circle the number that tells
how many there are.

Look at the number on each robot. Draw the correct number of knobs.

Example

Robot Math © 1989 David S. Lake Publishers

Name _____

Count the robots in each set. Cut out and then paste the number that tells how many there are.

Look at the number on each robot. Draw the correct number of knobs.

Example

Robot Math © 1989 David S. Lake Publishers

Count the robot faces in each set. Cut out and then paste the number that tells how many there are.

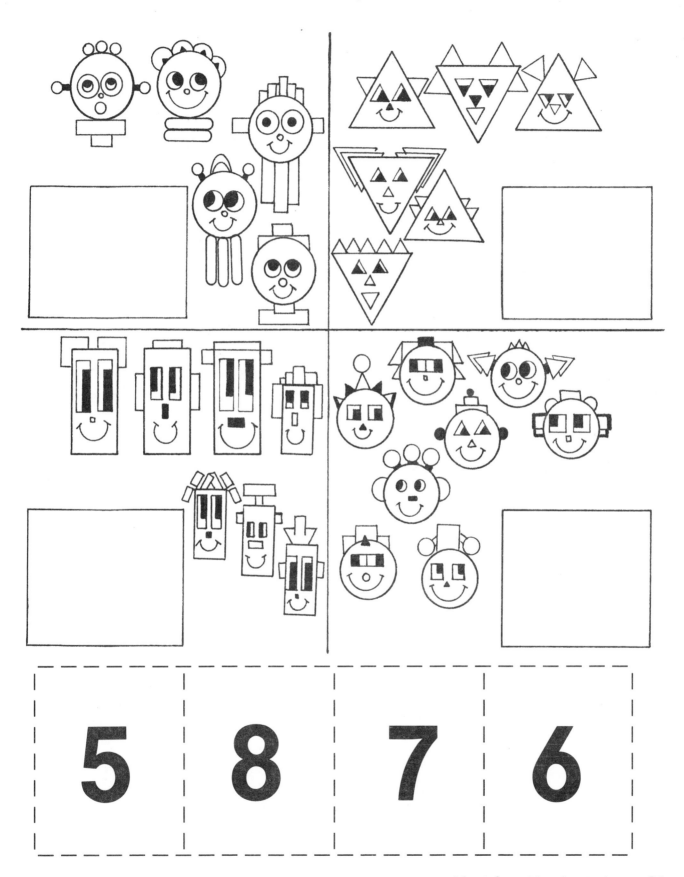

Name _____

Count the robots in each set. Circle the number that tells
how many there are.

5 6 7

6 7 8

7 8 9

8 9 10

Robot Math © 1989 David S. Lake Publishers

Name _____

Look at the number on each robot. Color the correct number of squares.

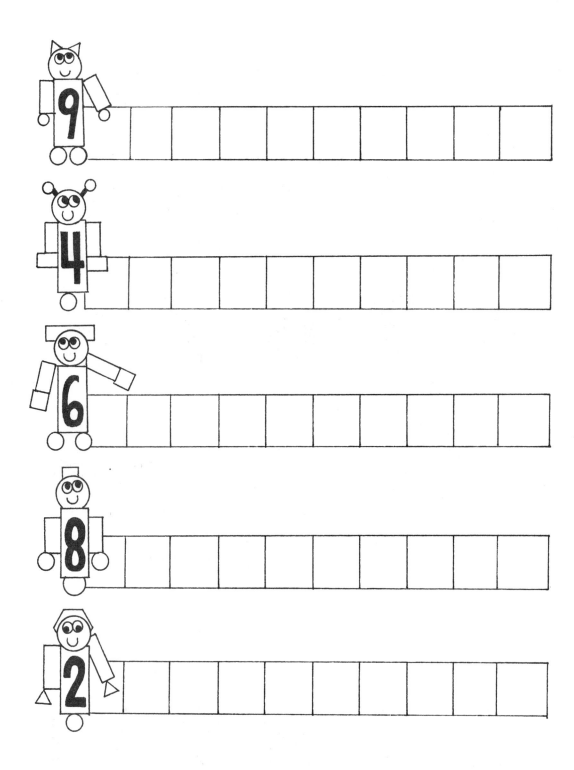

Name _____

Look at the number on each robot. Draw the same number of antennas.

Example

Robot Math © 1989 David S. Lake Publishers

Name _____

Count the feet on each robot. Write the number on its body.

Example

Name _____

Count the dots on each robot's chest. Write the number on its wheel.

Robot Math © 1989 David S. Lake Publishers

Name _____

Count the antennas (dots) on each robot's head. Write the number on its body.

Example

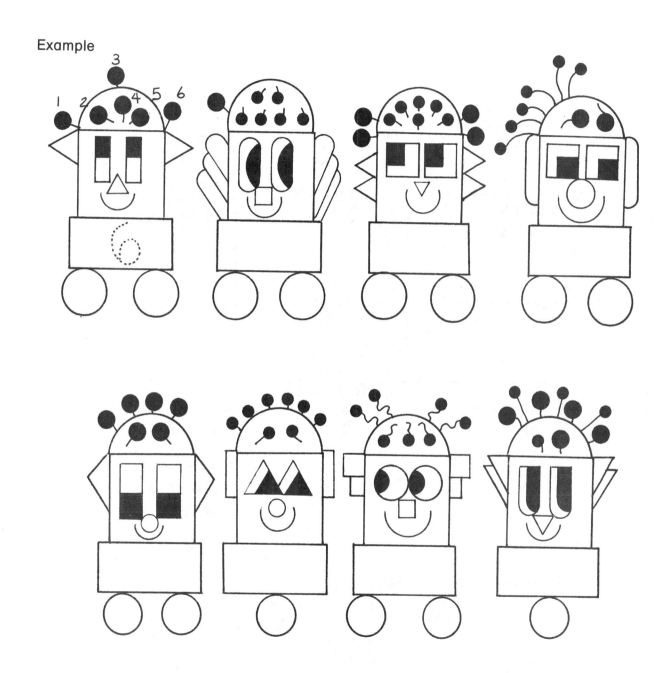

Name _____

Count the dots. Color the spaces. Use this color code:

● = blue

○ ○ = yellow

○ ○ ○ = orange

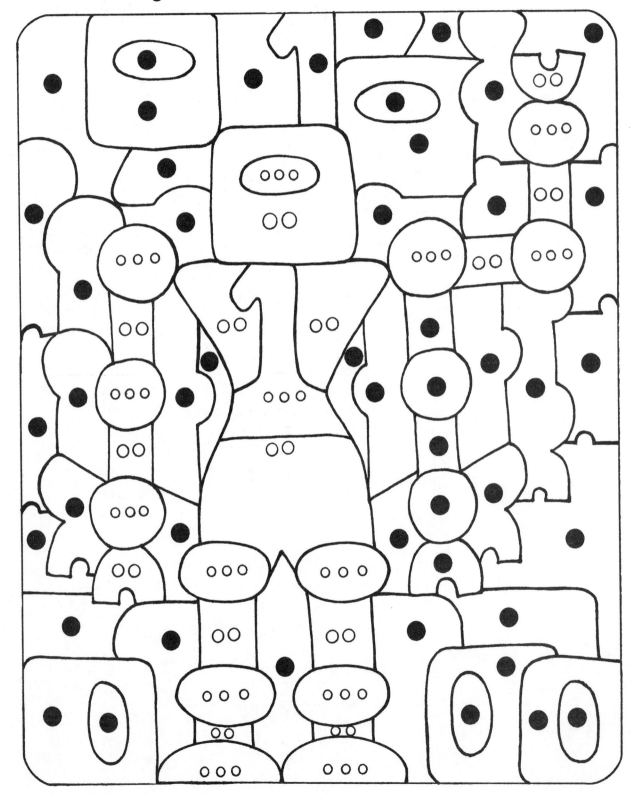

Robot Math © 1989 David S. Lake Publishers

Name _____

Count the dots. Color the spaces. Use this color code:

○ = orange   ○ ○ ○ = yellow   ○ ○ = green

○ ○ = brown   ○ ○

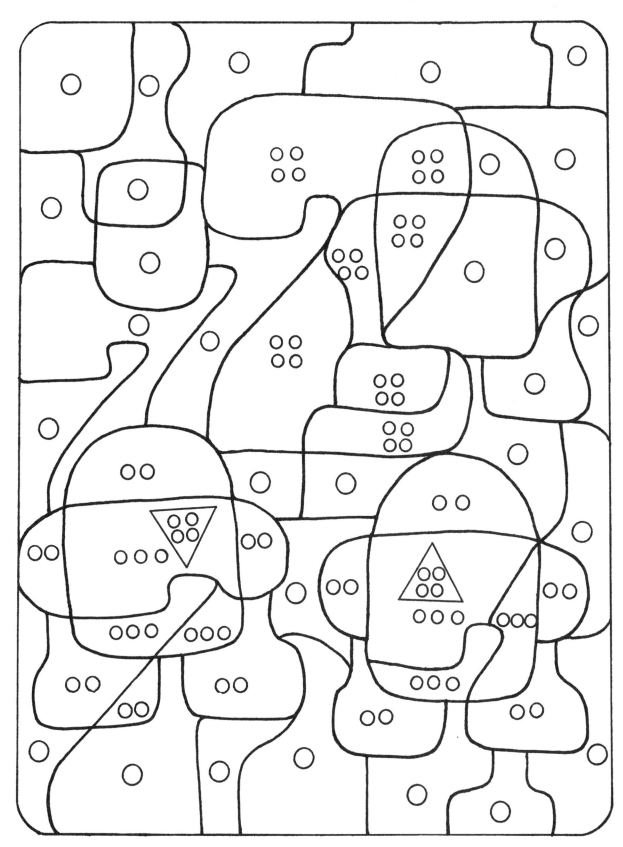

Name _____

Count the dots. Color the spaces. Use this color code:

● = yellow

● ● = blue

Robot Math © 1989 David S. Lake Publishers

Name _____

Count the dots. Color the spaces. Use this color code:

◯ = black

● ● = red   ● ● ● = blue

Count the dots. Color the spaces. Use this color code:

◯ = green   ● ● ● = pink

● ● = purple   ⦂⦂ = yellow

Robot Math © 1989 David S. Lake Publishers

Name _____

Color the spaces. Use this color code:

1 = orange

2 = purple

3 = blue

Name _____

Color the spaces. Use this color code:
1 = yellow
2 = pink
3 = blue

Robot Math © 1989 David S. Lake Publishers

Name _____

Color the spaces. Use this color code:
1 = blue
2 = brown
3 = orange
4 = yellow

Name _____

Color the spaces. Use this color code:

1 = yellow   4 = green
2 = orange   5 = purple
3 = brown

Robot Math © 1989 David S. Lake Publishers

Name _____

Color the spaces. Use this color code:
1 = black   4 = purple
2 = orange   5 = yellow
3 = green

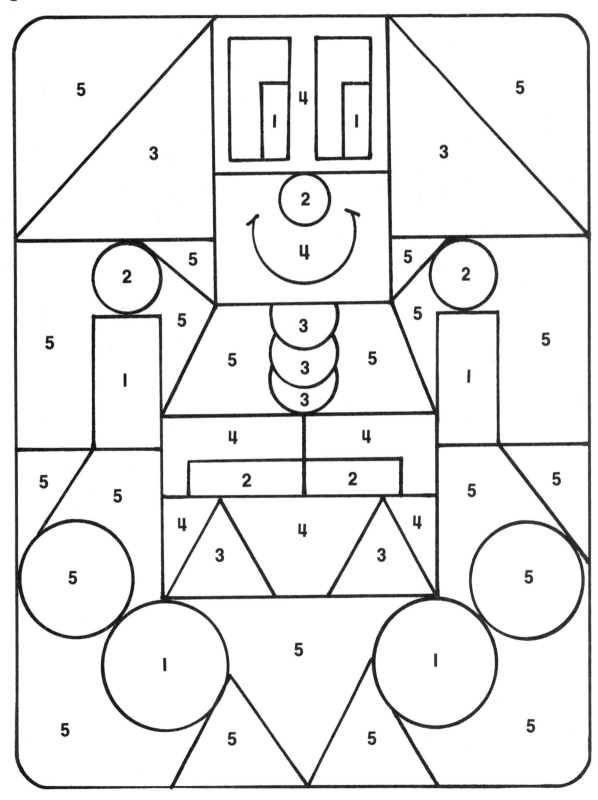

Name _____

Color the spaces. Use this color code:

6 = brown   9 = light green
7 = gray   10 = dark green
8 = orange

Robot Math © 1989 David S. Lake Publishers

Name _____

Color the spaces. Use this color code:

6 = red 9 = yellow
7 = blue 10 = green
8 = black

Name _____

Color the spaces. Use this color code:

5 = blue   8 = yellow
6 = red   9 = black
7 = orange   10 = gray

Robot Math © 1989 David S. Lake Publishers

Name _____

Color the spaces. Use this color code:

5 = blue   8 = red
6 = black   9 = orange
7 = gray   10 = yellow

Name _____

Color the spaces. Use this color code:

5 = red   8 = gray
6 = light blue   9 = black
7 = dark blue   10 = yellow

Robot Math © 1989 David S. Lake Publishers

Connect the dots from 1 to 10. Color the picture.

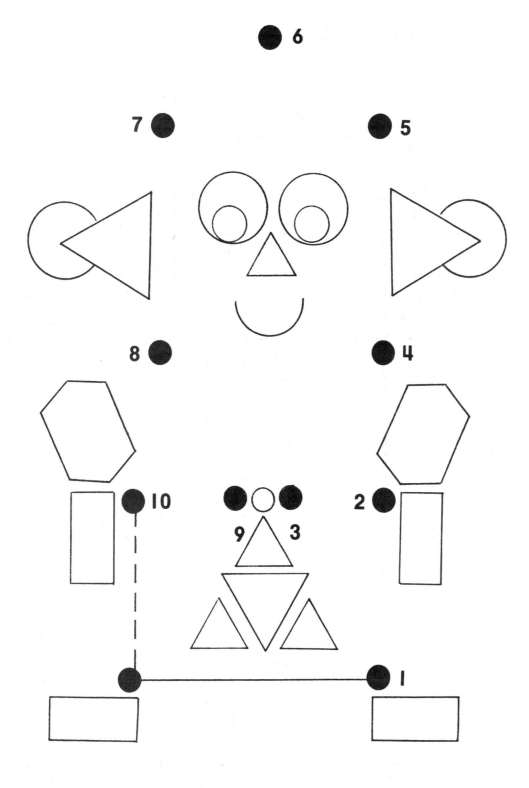

Connect the dots from 1 to 10. Color the picture.

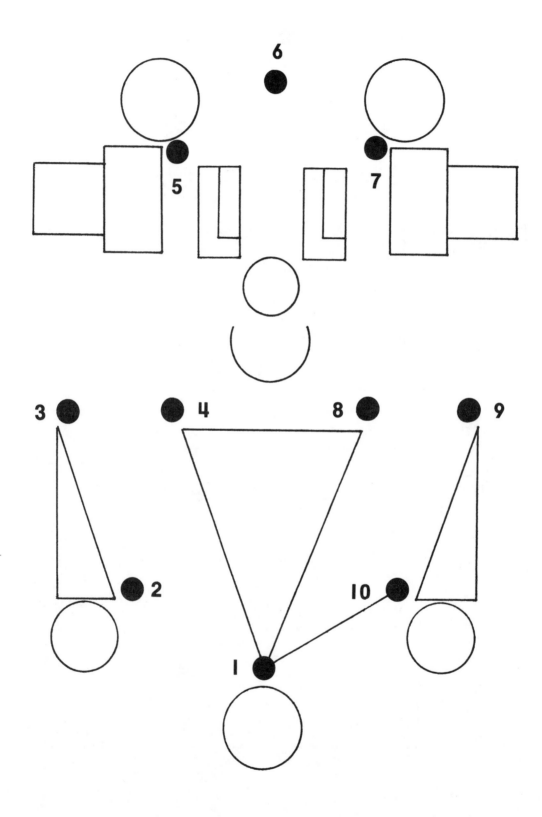

Robot Math © 1989 David S. Lake Publishers

Name _____

Connect the dots from 1 to 20. Color the picture.

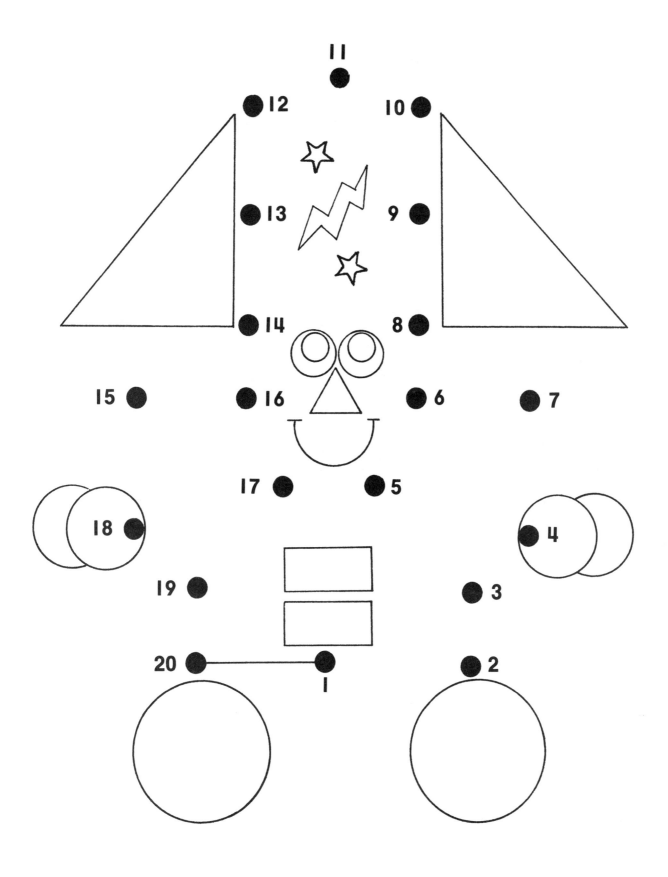

Name _____

Connect the dots from 1 to 20. Trace the dotted circles.
Color the picture.

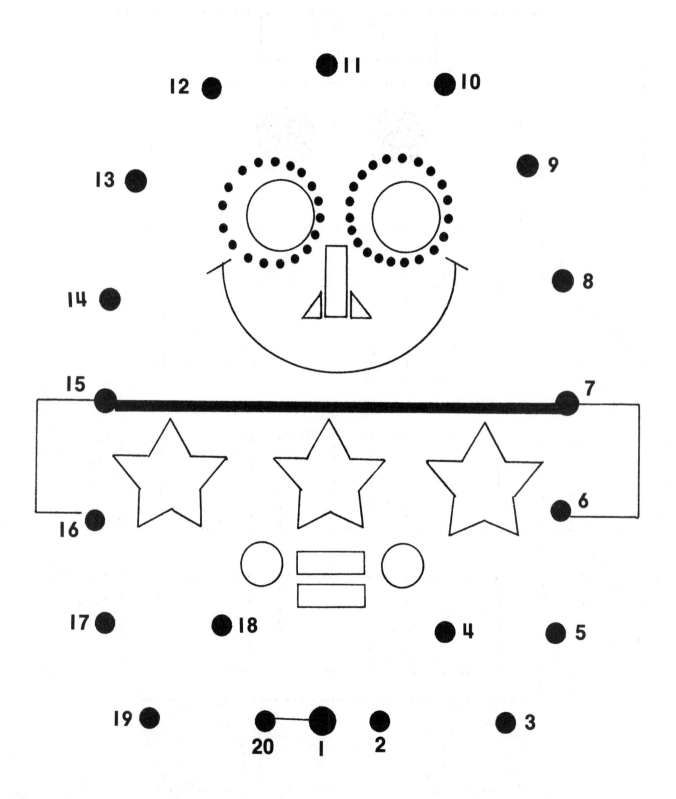

Robot Math © 1989 David S. Lake Publishers

Name _____

This is Telebot, the telephone robot. Trace his numbers and write in the missing ones.

Name _____

Write the missing numbers in the correct order.

Robot Math © 1989 David S. Lake Publishers

Name _____

Cut out the numbers. Paste them in order on the robots.

2 1 3 4 5

Name _____

Cut out the numbers. Paste them in order on the robots.

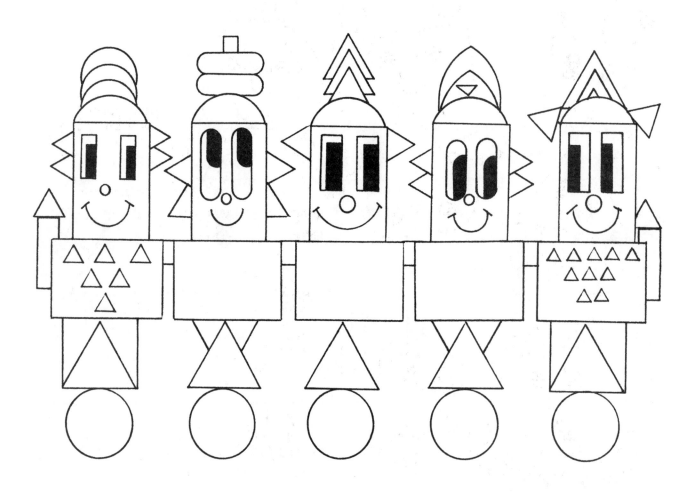

7   6   8   9   10

Robot Math © 1989 David S. Lake Publishers

Name _____

Write the missing numbers in the correct order.

Name _____

Cut out the numbers. Paste them in order on the robots.

Robot Math © 1989 David S. Lake Publishers

Marshmallow Robot Design Cards

Robot Math © 1989 David S. Lake Publishers

Marshmallow Robot Design Cards

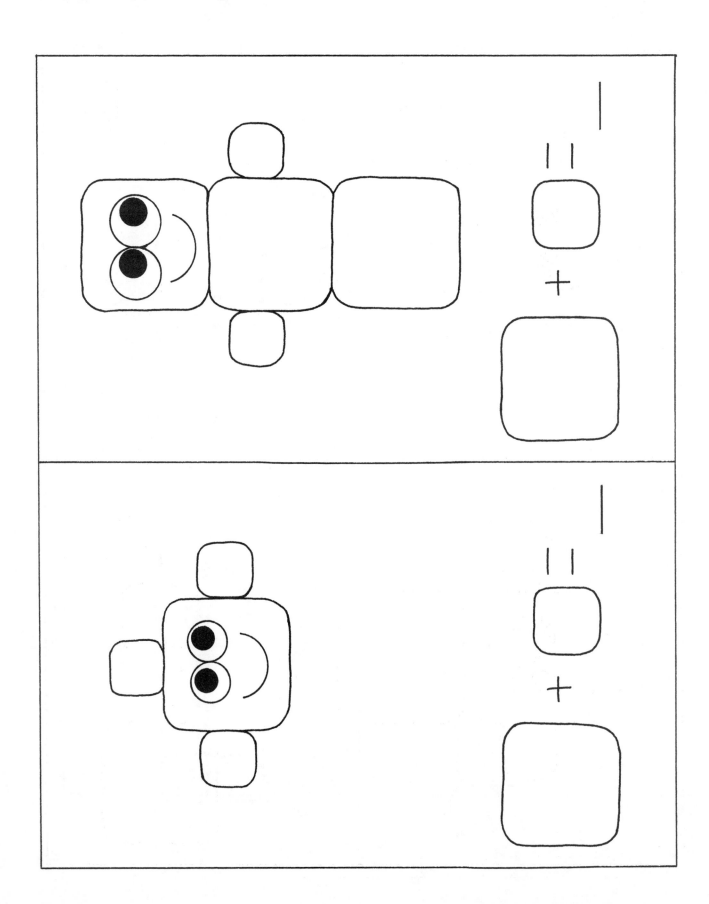

Robot Math © 1989 David S. Lake Publishers

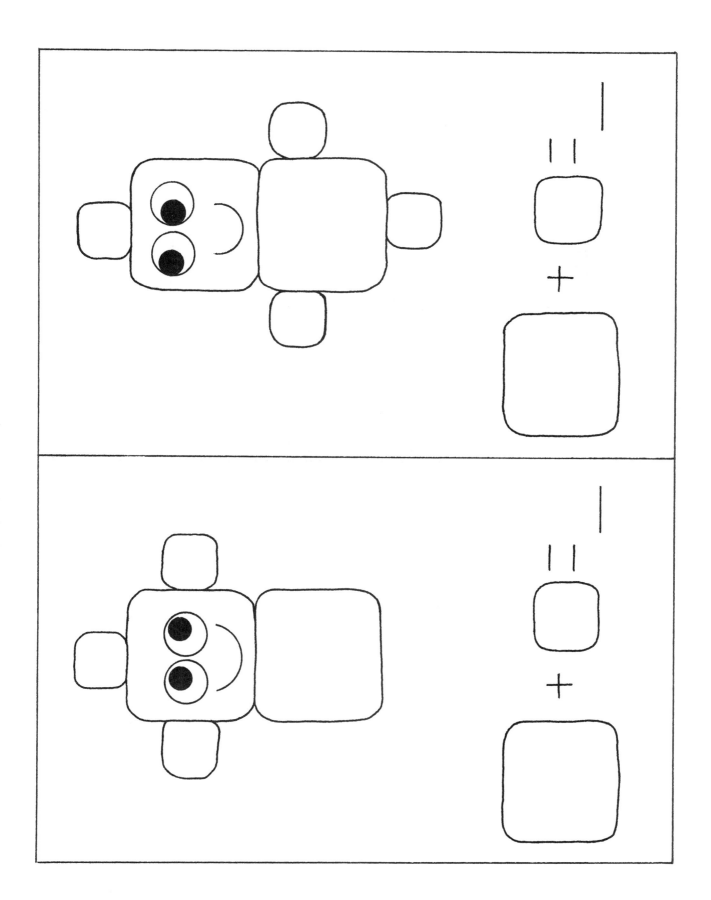

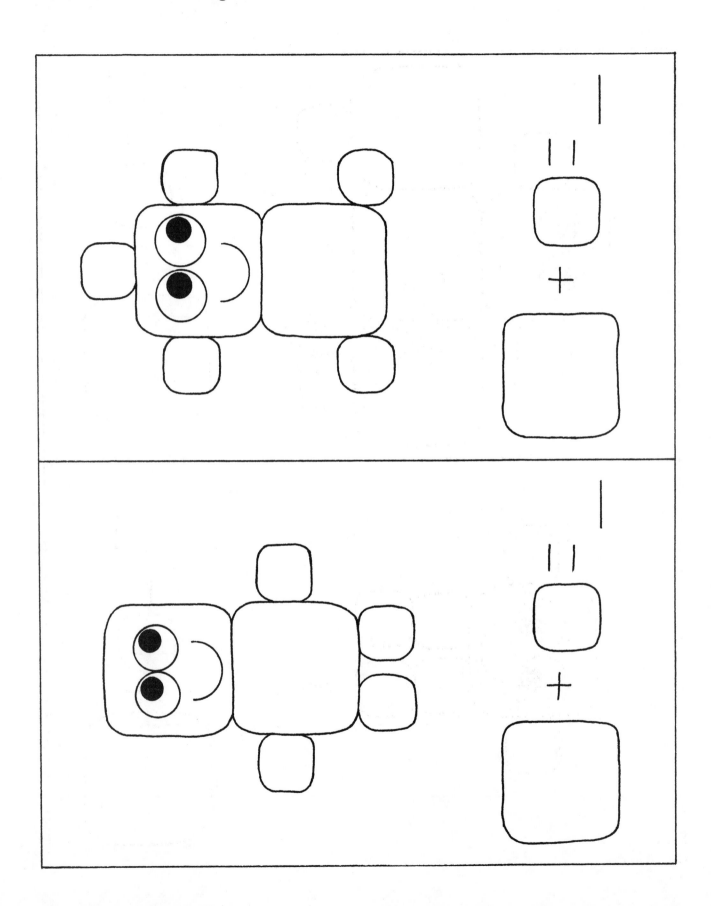

Robot Math © 1989 David S. Lake Publishers

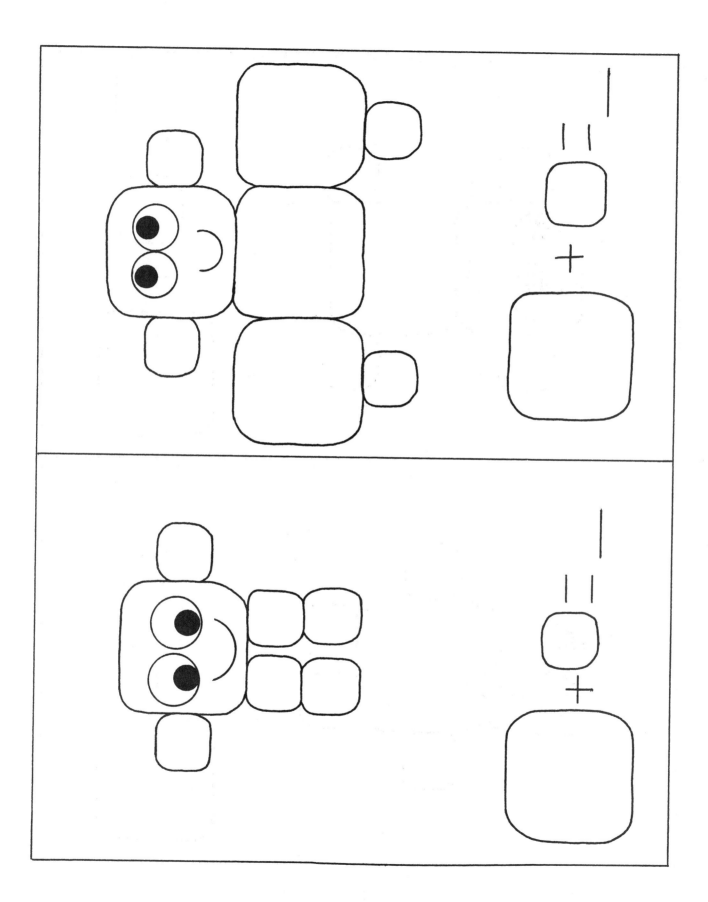

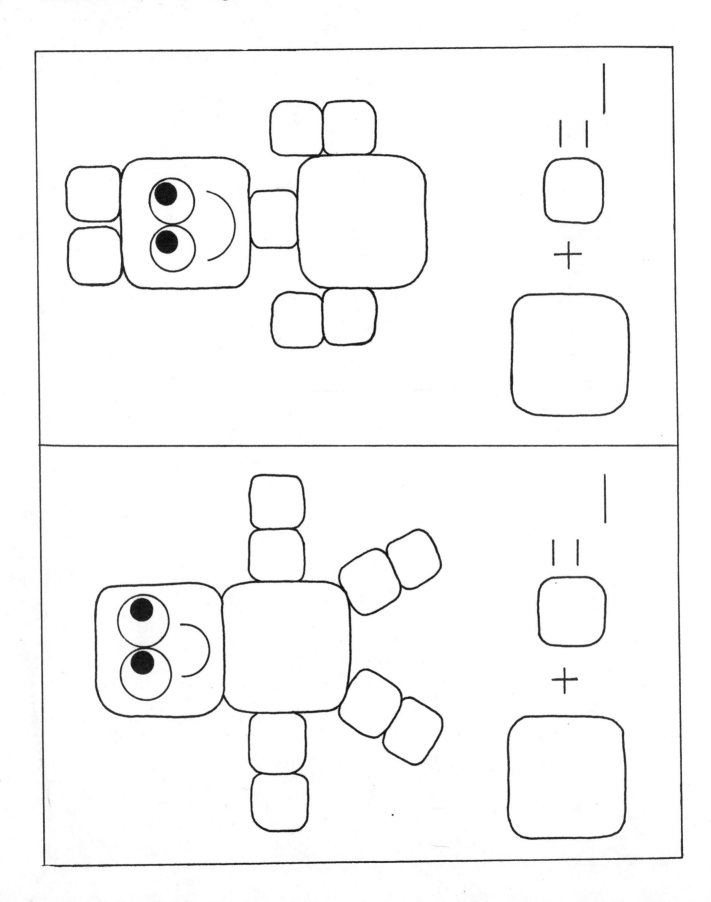

Robot Math © 1989 David S. Lake Publishers